AF575450

WILDFIRE SURVIVAL STORIES

BY JANIE HAVEMEYER

childsworld.com

Published by The Child's World®
800-599-READ • www.childsworld.com

Copyright © 2024 by The Child's World®
All rights reserved. No part of this book may be reproduced or utilized in any form or by any means without written permission from the publisher.

Photography Credits
Photographs ©: Hector Amezcua/The Sacramento Bee/AP Images, cover, 1; Christian Roberts-Olsen/Shutterstock Images, 5; Gabrielle Lurie/San Francisco Chronicle/AP Images, 6; Shutterstock Images, 8 (left), 8 (right), 15, 25 (top left), 25 (right), 25 (bottom left); Virrage Images/Shutterstock Images, 9; M. Yerman/Shutterstock Images, 11; Sam Mooy/Getty Images News/Getty Images, 12; Red Line Editorial, 14, 19, 28–29; Eric Paul Zamora/The Fresno Bee/AP Images, 16; David Aughenbaugh/Shutterstock Images, 18; iStockphoto, 20; Erik John Photography/Shutterstock Images, 22; Tom Reichner/Shutterstock Images, 24; Ian Dewar Photography/Shutterstock Images, 26

ISBN Information
9781503854529 (Reinforced Library Binding)
9781503854833 (Portable Document Format)
9781503855212 (Online Multi-user eBook)
9781503855595 (Electronic Publication)

LCCN 2023937274

Printed in the United States of America

ABOUT THE AUTHOR

Janie Havemeyer has written many books for young readers. She lives in San Francisco, California, and has seen many wildfires in her state. When Havemeyer is not writing, she likes to read, hike, spend time with her family, and travel.

CONTENTS

WHAT IS A WILDFIRE? 4
FAST FACTS 5

CHAPTER ONE
A SCHOOL BUS HERO 7

CHAPTER TWO
FIRE IN MALLACOOTA 12

CHAPTER THREE
A RING OF FIRE 16

CHAPTER FOUR
A LAST STAND 20

CHAPTER FIVE
DOWN THE MOUNTAIN 24

Think About It 27
Wildfire Map 28
Glossary 30
Selected Bibliography 31
Find Out More 31
Index 32

WHAT IS A WILDFIRE?

Wildfires, sometimes called bush or forest fires, are out-of-control fires that burn up natural areas such as forests and grasslands. Wildfires need the right conditions to start. First, an area needs to have plants such as grasses or trees. Second, the area must experience a hot and dry period. If a blaze starts under these conditions, it could easily and quickly spread, burning up the dry plants as it goes.

Lightning and human activities start wildfires. People may leave a match or campfire burning or **smoldering**. Wind may toss sparks and embers onto dry plants, which **ignite** into flames and spread.

The United States has many wildfires each year. However, only a small number become out of control. Catastrophic wildfires hurt plants and animals. They can also damage property, and people may die if caught in their path.

FAST FACTS

- The Camp Fire started on November 8, 2018, in northern California's Butte County. Eighty-five people died.
- The Mallacoota Bushfire was one of many fires in Australia between September 2019 and March 2020. Thirty-three people died from these fires.
- The Creek Fire in California started on September 4, 2020. It was **contained** by December 24.
- The Beachie Creek Fire began on August 16, 2020, in Oregon. It killed five people.
- The Bolt Creek Fire was first reported on September 10, 2022, in Washington State. By October, it had burned around 15,000 acres (6,070 ha).

CHAPTER ONE

A SCHOOL BUS HERO

Kevin McKay shut the door of his school bus with a loud clap. Behind him, 22 schoolchildren and two teachers sat in silence. McKay peered through his windshield. Dark smoke from the Camp Fire made it impossible to see ahead.

November 8, 2018, had started like any other day at California's Ponderosa Elementary School. But a huge wildfire had ignited at dawn in a remote canyon. The flames spread so fast that it was burning nearly 1 acre (.4 ha) per second. Now the fire was tearing toward Paradise, a town in northern California. People needed to get out of Ponderosa Elementary before it burned to the ground.

McKay had his bus ready, and students piled into it. Mary Ludwig was a second grade teacher at the school. She led students out of their classrooms and to the bus. Outside, burning bark tumbled through the air. The last child climbed on the bus.

◄ People tried to outrun the flames when fleeing Paradise, California.

McKay pleaded for help. He could not drive safely through fire without more adults to calm the children. So Ludwig and kindergarten teacher Abbie Davis jumped on board, too.

As McKay steered the bus onto the road, flames roared alongside it. Red and blue police lights shot past as officers rushed to help others. McKay glued his eyes to the road.

DEVASTATING CALIFORNIA WILDFIRES

California has experienced a lot of damage from wildfires. The top five wildfires in the state have killed a total of 176 people and destroyed more than 30,000 buildings.

Wildfire	Deaths	Buildings Destroyed
Griffith Park Fire (1933)	29	0
Tunnel-Oakland Hills Fire (1991)	25	2,900
Cedar Fire (2003)	15	2,820
Tubbs Fire (2017)	22	5,636
Camp Fire (2018)	85	18,804

▲ The Camp Fire moved fast. When it first started, it spread 7.8 miles (12.5 km) in just 45 minutes.

Ten-year-old Rowan Stovall turned to her five-year-old seatmate. "You'll see your mom and dad again," she said. It felt like the right thing to say, even though Rowan wasn't sure it was true. Still, she grabbed her seatmate's hand and whispered, "The bus isn't going to catch on fire. We are going to be okay; I promise."

By now the roads out of Paradise were choked with other cars trying to escape. McKay kept driving and trying new roads.

But they were all packed with vehicles. The inside of the bus was getting hot and smoky.

When the bus reached Roe Road, Ludwig pleaded with McKay not to take it. The road was dangerously narrow and lined with dead brush. A police officer was there and told them, “There’s no other way out.” Davis whispered, “I don’t think we are going to make it.” The teachers held hands and prayed as the bus sped down the road.

When the black sky faded to gray as they got farther from the fire, the teachers knew they would survive. It had taken five hours to drive 30 miles (48 km) to a safe location. Ludwig said, “We had the bus driver from heaven.”

Before it died out, the Camp Fire spread more than 153,000 acres (61,900 ha). It destroyed 18,000 buildings. Approximately 95 percent of the structures in Paradise were gone.

The Camp Fire devastated homes and left almost nothing behind. ►

CHAPTER TWO

FIRE IN MALLACOOTA

Eleven-year-old Finn Burns steered a small motorboat away from the beach near his seaside home in Mallacoota—a town in southeastern Australia. It was December 31, 2019. Next to him, his brother, Caleb, hugged the family dog while his mother, Allison, looked around in horror.

◄ **Australian firefighters had to battle flames and thick smoke.**

There were thousands of families sheltering on the town's beaches or in boats on the water. Some wore gas masks. Others huddled under blankets. An out-of-control bushfire was bearing down on Mallacoota.

Small fires had been burning along Australia's southeastern coast since late November. The government warned people to leave Mallacoota in December as the fires spread. Then on New Year's Eve, an emergency warning was issued for the Mallacoota area. It said, "It is too late to leave. Leaving now would be deadly." The town, packed with vacationers enjoying the holidays, was surrounded by fire. A giant column of smoke reached 8.7 miles (14 km) into the sky. It was so big that it made its own lightning. The only place to escape was by or on the water.

People in the area heard the bushfire approach. It sounded like a jet. Sirens rang out, and the black sky began to glow red from the flames. Hot embers swirled in the air. Soon trees caught fire. People fled to the water. Many of them watched the raging fire in numb silence. Amy Savage was in a boat on the water. She watched in terror. She wondered how bad the fire would be and how long they would be stuck on the water. "The scariest thing was not knowing," she said.

The crowds on the shore watched and waited, too. People planned a final escape. The water would be the safest place if the fire got closer. Flames began to burn up houses in the town. Then in the afternoon the wind shifted, and the fire changed direction. A cheer went up along the waterfront when news spread. Most of the town was spared. Then more good news arrived. Royal Australian Navy ships were on the way with food and water.

AUSTRALIA'S FIRES

The bushfires that started in late 2019 in Australia lasted for months. At some points, there were more than 100 fires raging across the country. On January 2, 2020, many parts of Australia were still battling the fires.

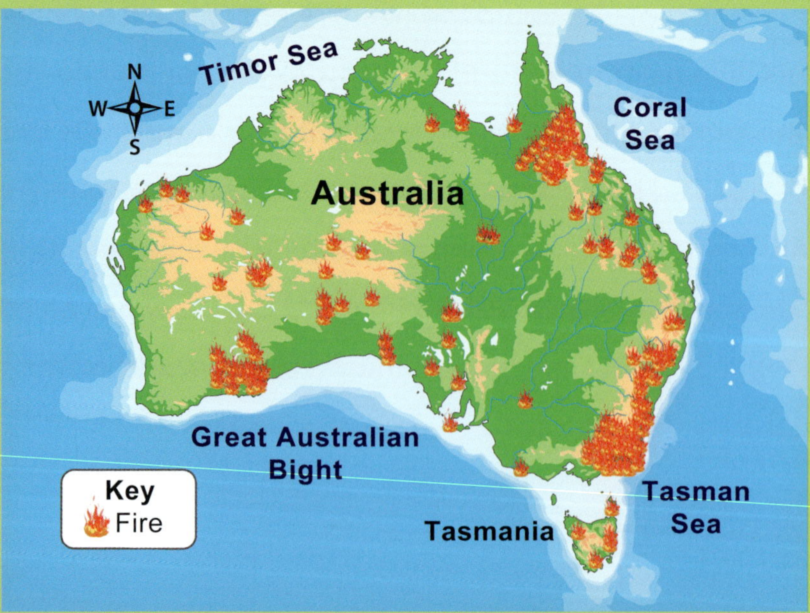

▲ **Kangaroo Island is in southern Australia, and fires ignited there in 2019. The disaster impacted animals such as kangaroos and koalas.**

They would rescue thousands of people. Deb Abbott was a police officer who helped the rescue effort. She said people survived because they worked together. "It's almost like times of war. . . . You see the best of people," she said.

More than 29 million acres (11.7 million ha) of forest and woodland burned during Australia's wildfires in late 2019 and early 2020. More than 3,000 homes were destroyed. Billions of animals were impacted.

CHAPTER THREE

A RING OF FIRE

It started with a ribbon of smoke rising out of Big Creek Canyon, California, in 2020. Sal Gonzalez wasn't aware that a small blaze was about to become an **inferno**. He drove to the Sierra National Forest on Saturday, September 5. It was Labor Day weekend, and many people were out enjoying themselves.

◀ **Experts think the Creek Fire was caused by a lightning strike.**

A pontoon boat bounced in a trailer behind his truck. Gonzalez's college friends crowded in beside him. The men were headed to Mammoth Pool **Reservoir**. The reservoir was crowded when they arrived. Gonzalez unhitched the boat so he and his friends could go fishing on the lake.

By the afternoon, the sky had turned a smoky orange. Gonzalez could see flames in the mountains, but they seemed far away. Soon hot ash started falling from the sky. The wind picked up and the waves rocked the boat. Gonzalez yelled to his friends that they should get in his truck and leave. But by the time they reached the parking lot, it was too late. A smoky ring of fire surrounded the reservoir. Flames blocked the exit road. The men were trapped.

Hundreds of people scrambled to gather their belongings before the fire consumed them. The heat was scorching. Ash got into Gonzalez's mouth and eyes. People waded into the water to escape the heat and embers. Gonzalez plunged into the water, too. He prayed for a miracle.

Gonzalez was shivering when darkness fell. He had been in the cold water a long time. The thick smoke made it hard to breathe. Time was running out. Then Gonzalez heard a humming sound. Two National Guard helicopters appeared in the sky.

▲ **People use helicopters to dump water onto forest fires.**

Kipp Goding was one of the pilots. "Every piece of vegetation as far as you could see around that lake was on fire," he said. But both choppers touched down safely.

People started cheering and rushing out of the water. Women, children, and people with burns from the hot ash climbed into the choppers first. But there wasn't enough room for everyone.

Gonzalez stayed behind. The pilots promised to return for the rest of them. Gonzalez knew he couldn't last much longer, but at least now there was hope.

It took a few more hours, but at 2:00 a.m. on Sunday, Gonzalez scrambled on board the last helicopter. It lifted him and dozens of others into the red sky. They were the last of the 214 passengers rescued from the Creek Fire. The fire burned more than 379,000 acres (153,376 ha), but no one lost their lives.

THE COST OF CALIFORNIA'S WILDFIRES

Each year, fires in California cost millions or billions of dollars to put out.

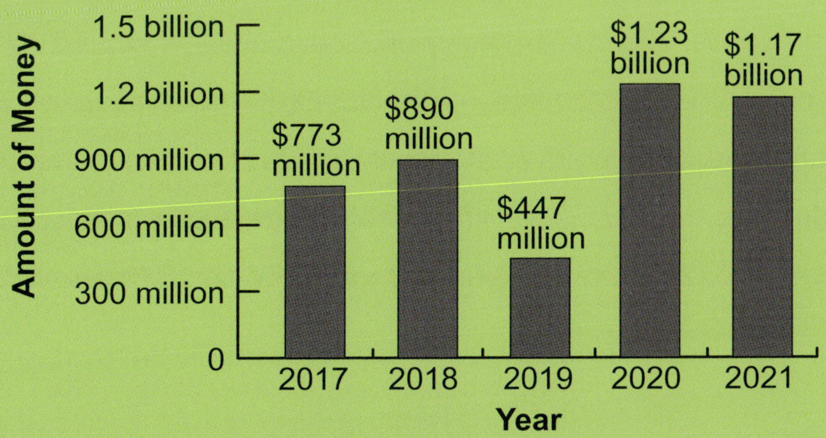

CHAPTER FOUR

A LAST STAND

Don Tesdal was a volunteer firefighter. He drove around town yelling, "Everybody, wake up! Fire! Fire!" The Beachie Creek Fire was coming over the mountain and heading to the small logging town of Detroit, Oregon. The fire had ignited on August 16, 2020, in Oregon's Willamette National Forest.

◄ **Smoke from wildfires can impact air quality and hurt people's health.**

It had started from a lightning strike. In September, powerful wind gusts spread the flames. Then that wildfire merged with another, becoming a monster inferno. By the early morning of September 8, the fire was charging toward Detroit.

Some residents were able to escape on the highway out of town. Along the way, they were hit with fiery pine cones and tree branches. Sometimes people had to climb from their cars and push fallen trees off the road. But when the fire circled the town and blocked roads, many people were trapped.

Kristy McMorlan and her husband had tried to escape, but a **rockslide** blocked the road they were on. They had no choice but to find a safe place to hide in Detroit. Firefighters told them to head to the reservoir for a helicopter rescue. The couple joined 80 other people down by the water. By now, ash fell like snow and the air was choked with smoke. McMorlan heard a helicopter's spinning blades in the air above. But then word arrived over the firefighters' radio: the helicopters could not land safely. They wouldn't be able to rescue anyone in the town. People trapped in Detroit needed to fight the Beachie Creek Fire if they wanted to stay alive.

▲ **Firefighters put themselves in harm's way to protect people.**

Volunteer firefighter Roberto DelaMontaigne organized the cutting and clearing of bushes and trees at the reservoir. He was building a **firebreak**. At the same time, people gathered food and water to help them survive the days ahead. Firefighters lined up their trucks as a barrier between the fire and people. They got ready to blast water at the flames until their water supply ran out. After that, everyone would float in the choppy waters of the half-filled reservoir.

Then a man from the US Forest Service arrived holding a map. He huddled with the firefighters. There was a chance of escape.

They could take a forest road. It had been cleared of fallen trees days earlier. DelaMontaigne started telling people, “Pack up your stuff! Let’s get out of here.”

Everyone piled into their cars and campers. A fire truck led them onto Forest Road 46. The way was thick with smoke. Flames roared on either side. But when McMorlan spotted blue sky, she said, “Oh, praise the Lord, we’re going to make it!”

TOP TEN STATES FOR WILDFIRES

In 2021, many western US states had high numbers of acres destroyed by wildfires.

State	Land Burned
California	2.2 million acres (890,308 ha)
Oregon	828,777 acres (335,394 ha)
Montana	747,678 acres (302,575 ha)
Washington	674,222 acres (272,848 ha)
Arizona	524,428 acres (212,229 ha)
Idaho	439,600 acres (177,900 ha)
Alaska	253,357 acres (102,530 ha)
Texas	168,258 acres (68,090 ha)
Kansas	163,982 acres (66,361 ha)
Nevada	127,427 acres (51,568 ha)

CHAPTER FIVE

DOWN THE MOUNTAIN

When Matt Bishop reached the **ridge**, he saw flames in the distance. "We need to get out of here," he yelled to his best friend, Steve Cooper. The two hikers had set out on September 10, 2022, to hike up Baring Mountain in Washington. They left at dawn, as they always did on their hiking adventures.

◄ **Large wildfires can be seen from miles away.**

At that time, the sky had been mostly clear. Neither man knew a fire had started just a few miles away from them. After six hours of hiking, the friends now had a clear view of the massive Bolt Creek Fire about 3 or 4 miles (4.8 to 6.4 km) away. It was moving like a speeding train toward them.

CLIMATE CHANGE AND WILDFIRES

People burn **fossil fuels**. The gases that these fuels give off have warmed Earth, causing climate change. In some areas, climate change is leading to less rain and warmer weather. These conditions make it easier for wildfires to start and spread.

Weather is getting warmer
Between 1970 and 2014, temperatures increased almost 2 degrees F (1 degree C) in the western United States.

Warmer weather causes snow to melt almost one month earlier.

Warmer weather and faster snowmelt mean forests are drier for longer stretches of time, putting them at risk for out-of-control wildfires.

▲ **The Bolt Creek Fire left some mountainous areas looking like wastelands.**

Cooper and Bishop raced down the mountain. But soon the fire was in front of them, and the trail they had hiked up was ablaze with flames. Smoke filled the air. "We're probably not going to make this," said Cooper. Bishop called 911 for help and was connected to the sheriff. The sheriff told them the bad news. It was too risky to get a helicopter there to rescue them. They would have to find another way down the mountain.

As the heat and smoke from the flames got worse. Cooper and Bishop covered their mouths with scarves. They checked the GPS on their cell phones, praying it would help guide them to safety. The ground was slippery with ash as they scrambled downhill.

They followed a steep **ravine**, keeping an eye on the flames. The two friends crept along narrow ledges with dangerous drop-offs. Then Bishop's foot slipped and he fell, sliding toward the edge of a cliff that had a 200-foot (61-m) drop. Bishop grabbed a tree branch and steadied himself. It was a lucky break that saved his life.

The men continued hurrying downhill, answering calls from the sheriff and a 911 operator as they went. The phone support gave them courage to keep moving. At last, Cooper and Bishop saw a familiar trail. It had taken four hours of climbing down rock ledges and crawling over fallen trees and boulders to get to this spot. But now they knew it would be an easy hike to their jeep. Determination, luck, and the hope of seeing their families again had helped them survive the wildfire.

THINK ABOUT IT

- What can people do to prevent wildfires from starting and spreading?
- What can you do to help people who have been impacted by wildfires?
- You might not live in an area that is at risk for wildfires. Do you still think it's important to learn about them? Explain your answer.

WILDFIRE MAP

WESTERN UNITED STATES

PACIFIC OCEAN
INDIAN OCEAN
AUSTRALIA
Mallacoota Bushfire
(2019 to 2020)
N
W
E
S

GLOSSARY

contained (kun-TAYND): Contained means to have controlled or stopped the spread. Firefighters contained the wildfire.

firebreak (FIRE-brayk): A firebreak is a barrier of cleared land that helps to stop a fire from spreading. Firefighters made a firebreak to save the town.

fossil fuels (FOSS-uhl FYOO-uhls): Fossil fuels are sources of energy that come from the remains of plants and animals that died long ago. Coal, oil, and natural gas are fossil fuels.

ignite (ig-NITE): Ignite means to set on fire. Dry plants may ignite from a few sparks.

inferno (in-FUR-no): An inferno is an intense and raging fire. The small fire had grown into an inferno.

ravine (ruh-VEEN): A ravine is a deep, narrow valley with steep sides. The hikers went into the ravine.

reservoir (REZ-ur-vwar): A reservoir is a natural or human-made lake used to store large amounts of water. People jumped into the reservoir to escape the fire.

ridge (RIJ): A ridge is a range of mountains or a raised strip. The hiker stood on the ridge to get a better view.

rockslide (RAHK-slide): A rockslide is when large rocks fall down a hill. The road was blocked by a rockslide.

smoldering (SMOHL-dur-ing): When something is smoldering, it has smoke but no flames. The fire was started by a smoldering campfire.

SELECTED BIBLIOGRAPHY

Healy, Jack, and Mike Baker. "A Desperate Bid for Survival as Fire Closed in on an Oregon Mountain Town." *New York Times*, 19 Sept. 2020, nytimes.com. Accessed 15 Mar. 2023.

Johnson, Lizzie. *Paradise: One Town's Struggle to Survive an American Wildfire*. New York, NY: Crown, 2021.

FIND OUT MORE

BOOKS

Adamson, Thomas K., and Heather Adamson. *California Wildfires Survival Stories*. Parker, CO: The Child's World, 2016.

Potenza, Alessandra. *All about Wildfires*. New York, NY: Children's Press, 2021.

Seigel, Rachel. *California and Other Western Wildfires*. New York, NY: Crabtree Publishing, 2019.

WEBSITES

Visit our website for links about wildfires:
childsworld.com/links

Note to Parents, Caregivers, Teachers, and Librarians: We routinely verify our Web links to make sure they are safe and active sites. So encourage your readers to check them out!

INDEX

Abbott, Deb, 15

Baring Mountain, 24–27
Beachie Creek Fire, 5, 20–23
Bishop, Matt, 24–27
boat, 12–13, 17
Bolt Creek Fire, 5, 24–27
Burns, Finn, 12

Camp Fire, 5, 7–10
climate change, 25
contained, 5
Cooper, Steve, 24–27
Creek Fire, 5, 16–19

Davis, Abbie, 8, 10
DelaMontaigne, Roberto, 22–23
Detroit, Oregon, 20–23

firebreak, 22
firefighters, 20–22
fossil fuels, 25

Goding, Kipp, 18
Gonzalez, Sal, 16–19

helicopters, 17–19, 21, 26
hiking, 24–27

ignite, 4, 7, 20
inferno, 16, 21

Ludwig, Mary, 7–8, 10

Mallacoota Bushfire, 5, 12–15
Mammoth Pool Reservoir, 17
McKay, Kevin, 7–10
McMorlan, Kristy, 21, 23

National Guard, 17

Paradise, California, 7–10
Ponderosa Elementary School, 7

ravine, 27
ridge, 24
Royal Australian Navy, 14

Savage, Amy, 13
Sierra National Forest, 16
smoldering, 4
snowmelt, 25

Tesdal, Don, 20

US Forest Service, 22

Willamette National Forest, 20